This book belongs to:

....

Easy-Peasy Recipes

Snacks & Treats to Make & Eat

Recipes and text by Karen Berman

Illustrations by Doreen M. Marts

Edited by Kirsten Hall

RP | KIDS

PHILADELPHIA • LONDON

Printed in China

Books published by Running Press are available at special discounts for bulk
purchases in the United States by corporations, institutions, and other organi-
zations. For more information, please contact the Special Markets Department
at the Perseus Books Group, 2300 Chestnut Street, Suite 200, Philadelphia, PA
19103, or call (800) 810-4145, ext. 5000, or e-mail special.markets@
perseusbooks.com.

ISBN 978-0-7624-4443-4

Library of Congress Control Number: 2011937816

E-book ISBN 978-0-7624-4534-9

9 8 7 6 5 4 3 2 1
Digit on the right indicates the number of this printing

Cover and interior design by Ryan Hayes
Edited by Kirsten Hall
Typography: Clarendon and Burbank

Published by Running Press Kids
An Imprint of Running Press Book Publishers
A Member of the Perseus Books Group
2300 Chestnut Street
Philadelphia, PA 19103–4371

Visit us on the web!
www.runningpress.com

For Jessica and Anna.–K. B.

Acknowledgments

A big giant thank-you to my wonderful daughter, Jessica, for helping to develop these recipes and testing and tasting them. Another big thank-you to my sweet niece Anna, for testing and tasting. Thanks also to our friends Jolie Patten, Rena Patten, Sara Morgan Block, and Shoshana Lieberman.—K. B.

Recipes

Introduction

Hi, Kids,

Putting together a yummy, healthful snack is easy-peasy, especially when you have recipes to guide you. All the recipes in this book are for kids! You won't need to use the stove, the oven, or sharp knives. (A few of the recipes call for foods that have already been cooked—be sure to ask a grown-up for help with those.)

One thing you do have to know is how to measure—in other words, how much of each food to add. Here are some tips for measuring.

Measuring spoons are used for small amounts of ingredients, both wet (like juice or oil) and dry (like salt). They usually have a number on the handle to tell you how much they hold.

Measuring cups are used for large amounts. Wet ingredients are measured in a clear glass or plastic cup with little lines and numbers on the side. Dry ingredients that are made up of many pieces, like popcorn or green peas, are measured in a cup with a number on the handle to tell how much it holds. A dry measuring cup can be metal or plastic or ceramic, and it can be any color.

Dipping in Fruit Juice: Some of the recipes in this book ask you to dip apples or bananas into fruit juice. This is because these fruits turn brown when exposed to the air. The juice stops the browning.

Another Thing to Remember: Always wash your hands before you start to cook!

And above all . . . have fun!

Karen Berman

Tic-Tac-Toe Open-Faced Sandwich

Sometimes it's hard to stop playing, even if you're hungry. Here's a snack that lets you play and eat!
Makes 1 sandwich

Special Tools You Will Need

Safety scissors, washed and dried

Ingredients

1 slice of whole wheat bread

1 slice of cheese

5 round slices of cucumber

10 pieces of thinly shredded carrot

1. First, make your tic-tac-toe board with the slice of bread. With the scissors, use 2 cuts to make 3 long strips about the same size. Then make 2 cuts in each strip to make 3 squares. You will end up with 9 squares.

2. Put all the squares back together to make 1 big square.

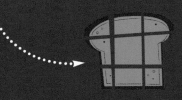

3. With scissors, make 9 squares out of the slice of cheese. Put 1 small square of cheese on each square of bread. Your tic-tac-toe board is made!

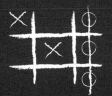

4. Use the cucumber slices for O. Overlap 2 pieces of carrot to make an X. Then make 4 more.

5. Play tic-tac-toe! Take turns until you have a winner. Then eat everything up!

Do It Another Way

You can use soy cheese or turkey breast or just plain bread; use grape tomatoes, green peas, green and purple grapes, or whatever veggies or fruits you like.

EASY-PEASY CHEESY POPCORN

Vegetable oil cooking spray

INGREDIENTS

6 cups of popcorn

¼ cup of grated Parmesan cheese

Special Tools You Will Need

A roasting pan or large bowl

Measuring cup

A paper towel

This cheesy popcorn is coated with real cheese, which is good for your bones!

Makes 4 to 6 easy-peasy cheesy servings

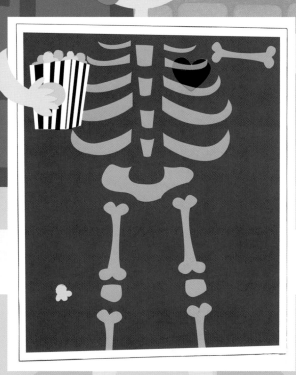

1. Spray the bottom of the roasting pan or bowl with the oil spray. Spread it around with a paper towel.

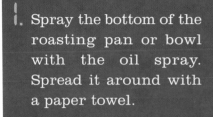

2. Measure 6 cups of popcorn, 1 at a time, and pour them into the pan or bowl.

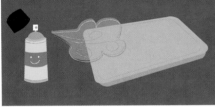

3. Sprinkle ¼ cup of grated cheese all over the popcorn. Then mix it with your hands. Do this **very gently**, or it will fly all over the place. Add a little more cheese if you want to. Eat up!

Do It Another Way

You can use cinnamon sugar, garlic salt, your favorite spice blend, or a few drops of hot sauce.

X-RAY VIEW-A-TRON 3000

CAPTAIN TACOSALAD

Special Tools You Will Need

A plastic knife

A dinner plate

Safety scissors, washed and dried

Measuring cup and spoons

Meet the famous pirate, Captain TacoSalad, the yummiest pirate to sail the seven seas!

Makes 1 yummy pirate lunch or light supper

Do It Another Way

You can add salad dressing, salsa, or guacamole to Captain TacoSalad's hat. Use different veggies for the face. You can also add cooked shredded chicken or seasoned ground beef or turkey to the tortilla. A hard-cooked egg, cut in half, makes good eyes. For a lady pirate, put some carrot sticks, celery sticks, or scallions on either side of the plate for hair.

INGREDIENTS

9 grape tomatoes

12 black olive slices

BLACK OLIVES

1 baby carrot

2 tablespoons of shredded carrots

¼ cup of shredded cheddar cheese

1 flour tortilla

2 pretty leaves of Romaine lettuce, 1 small and 1 large

First make Captain Taco-Salad's hat. Place the tortilla on the dinner plate. Pour ¼ cup of shredded cheese over half of the tortilla. Leave an empty space as wide as your finger around the edge, so you will be able to fold it without spilling everything, but don't fold it yet!

 Now pick up the side of the tortilla with nothing on it, and fold it over the cheese and vegetables to make a half circle. Move the plate so that the empty side is closest to you. With the fold of the tortilla facing your belly, put the small lettuce leaf on one side of the tortilla to make a feather for his hat.

2. Roll the large lettuce leaf into a log. With the scissors, cut it into thin pieces to make shredded lettuce. Scatter them over the cheese.

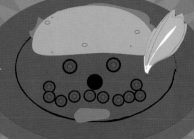 It's time for the captain's face. Put 2 olives on the plate where the eyes would be. Put the half of the tomato where the nose would be. Line up 5 olive slices on each side of the nose to make a long, curly mustache. Put the baby carrot where the mouth would be. Now say, "Arrrrrrgh!" and eat!

3. Scatter 2 tablespoons of shredded carrots over the lettuce.

4. With the plastic knife, cut the tomatoes in half. Set 1 half aside. Scatter the others on top of the lettuce and carrots.

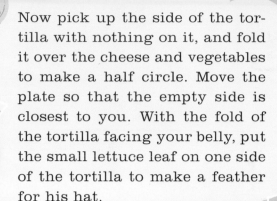

14

COLD CREEPY CRAWLY NOODLES

Did you ever eat worms? Spiders? Beetles? Close your eyes when you take a bite and use your imagination!

INGREDIENTS

1 tablespoon of soy sauce

SPAGHETTI

½ box of spaghetti, cooked and chilled

HOISIN SAUCE

(from the Asian food aisle in the supermarket)

⅓ cup of hoisin sauce

Makes 4 to 6 bowls of cold creepy crawlies

¼ cup of crispy chow mein noodles

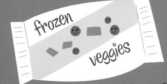
frozen veggies

1 cup of mixed frozen vegetables, such as peas, carrots, corn, and lima beans, thawed

2 tablespoons of chopped peanuts

⅓ cup of fresh bean sprouts

Special Tools You Will Need

A large mixing bowl

Measuring cup and spoons

A wooden spoon

15

Put the spaghetti in the large mixing bowl. Sprinkle 1 tablespoon of soy sauce over the spaghetti. Pour 1/3 cup of hoisin sauce over the spaghetti. Mix gently with the wooden spoon until all the spaghetti is light brown. These are your worms.

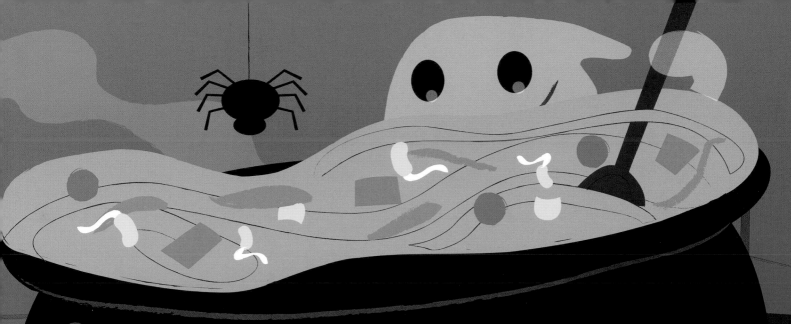

2. Pour 1 cup of mixed vegetables and ⅓ cup of bean sprouts into the spaghetti, and mix gently with the wooden spoon until there are vegetables all throughout the noodles. These are your bugs.

3. Sprinkle 2 tablespoons of peanuts and ¼ cup of crispy noodles on top. Mix gently. These are beetles and spiders.

4. Spoon some noodles into each serving bowl. Close your eyes and take a bite. Is that what worms and bugs taste like?

Do It Another Way

You can use any bite-size frozen vegetables—green beans, broccoli florets, or sugar snap peas. Add sunflower seeds, pumpkin seeds, or sesame seeds. If you like a

PRINCESS FRUITSALAD

Meet Princess FruitSalad. She's so sweet, you could eat her up!

Makes 2 to 4 fruity snacks

Special Tools You Will Need

Measuring cup

A shallow soup bowl

A plastic knife

A dinner plate

Do It Another Way

If you can't find dried mangoes, blueberries alone will make fine eyes. In fact, use any fruits you like for a yummy fruit salad.

Ingredients

1 banana

¼ cup of orange juice

1 apple wedge

10 blueberries

4 large strawberries

2 dried mango slices with nice flat sides

1 grape

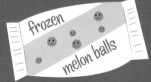

5 frozen melon balls, thawed

1. Measure ½ cup of juice into the bowl. Put the apple wedge into the juice. Turn it so the juice coats all sides. Take it out of the juice and set aside.

2. Peel the banana. With the plastic knife, cut it in half, the long way, to make 2 long, curved pieces. Put them into the juice. Turn them so the juice coats all sides. Take them out of the juice and set aside.

3. With the plastic knife, cut the leaves off the strawberries to make flat tops. Then cut them in half to make 2 triangles each.

4. Put 1 piece of banana on the right-hand side of the plate. Put the other piece on the left-hand side. This is the princess's hair.

5. Put the strawberry halves on the top of the plate with the points turned outward. This is the princess's crown.

6. Put 2 blueberries on the plate where the eyes would be. Put 1 mango slice above each blueberry eye. Put the grape where the nose would be. Use the apple wedge to make a smile. Decorate the crown with the rest of the fruit. Your royal fruit salad is served!

SNOWCAPPED MOUNTAIN*

Berries and cream (actually vanilla yogurt!) go mountain climbing in this tasty treat.

Special Tools You Will Need

Measuring cup and spoons

Safety scissors, washed and dried

A dessert plate

Makes 1 mountain snack or dessert

Ingredients

¼ cup of blueberries or raspberries

1 slice of whole wheat-raisin or regular raisin bread

¼ cup of regular or low-fat vanilla yogurt

1 teaspoon of sweetened shredded coconut

1. With the scissors, cut the bread in half from one corner to the other to make 2 triangles. Cut each triangle in half. You will have 4 triangles.

2. Spoon 2 tablespoons of vanilla yogurt onto the center of a dessert plate.

5. Spoon the rest of the yogurt on top of the mountain. Let it slide down the bread like snow.

3. Pile ¼ cup of berries on top of the yogurt to make a small mountain.

6. Sprinkle 1 teaspoon of shredded coconut on top of the yogurt. Let your spoon do the climbing while you do the eating!

4. Place the bread triangles on top of the berries in the shape of a pyramid. This is your mountain.

Do It Another Way

You can use cinnamon bread, wheat berry, or other sweet bread. Or cut small slices of banana bread, carrot cake, or zucchini bread and prop them together over the berries.

DiG THiS PiNeAPPLe PaRFaiT

Special Tools You Will Need

If you like to dig, this layered dessert is for you!
Makes 2 parfaits

A large fine-mesh strainer or colander

2 bowls

2 clear wine or other glasses

Measuring cup and spoons

A small saucepan with a handle

A large plastic zipper bag

A spoon

Ingredients

4 graham crackers

1 tablespoon of melted unsalted butter, cooled

26 canned pineapple chunks and their juice

About ¼ cup of regular or low-fat vanilla yogurt

Put the strainer or colander over one of the bowls. Pour in the pineapple chunks and juice. Lift up the strainer and set it aside with the fruit in it. Pour 3 tablespoons of the juice from the bowl into the other bowl. Pour in the melted butter and mix well.

Do It Another Way

You can use any canned fruit packed in its juice or pudding or frozen yogurt.

2. Put the graham crackers into the plastic bag. Seal it well. Holding the pot handle with both hands, bang on the bag with the bottom of the pot to make fine crumbs. Pour the crumbs into the butter and juice. Stir until all the crumbs look like wet sand. If they are too dry, pour in 1 more tablespoon of juice and mix again.

3. Put 5 pineapple chunks into the glass. Spoon 1 tablespoon of crumbs over the pineapple. Spoon 2 tablespoons of yogurt on top of the crumbs. Do it again with 5 more pineapple chunks, 1 more tablespoon of crumbs, and 2 more tablespoons of yogurt. Top with 3 pineapple chunks.

4. Make another parfait with the other glass and more pineapple, crumbs, and yogurt. Now dig in!

ANTS IN A LOG

You've probably tried Ants on a Log–peanut butter, celery, and raisins. But what about ants *in* a log? And not just black ants, but red ones, too?

Makes 1 ant-filled log (enough for a big snack, a nice lunch, or a light supper)

Do It Another Way

You can use sunflower butter and dried cherries or blueberries or any small or chopped dried fruit.

Ingredients

Softened peanut butter or softened low-fat or regular cream cheese

1 flour tortilla

Raisins

Raisins

Dried cranberries

Special Tools You Will Need

A spoon

1 plastic knife or other spreader

26

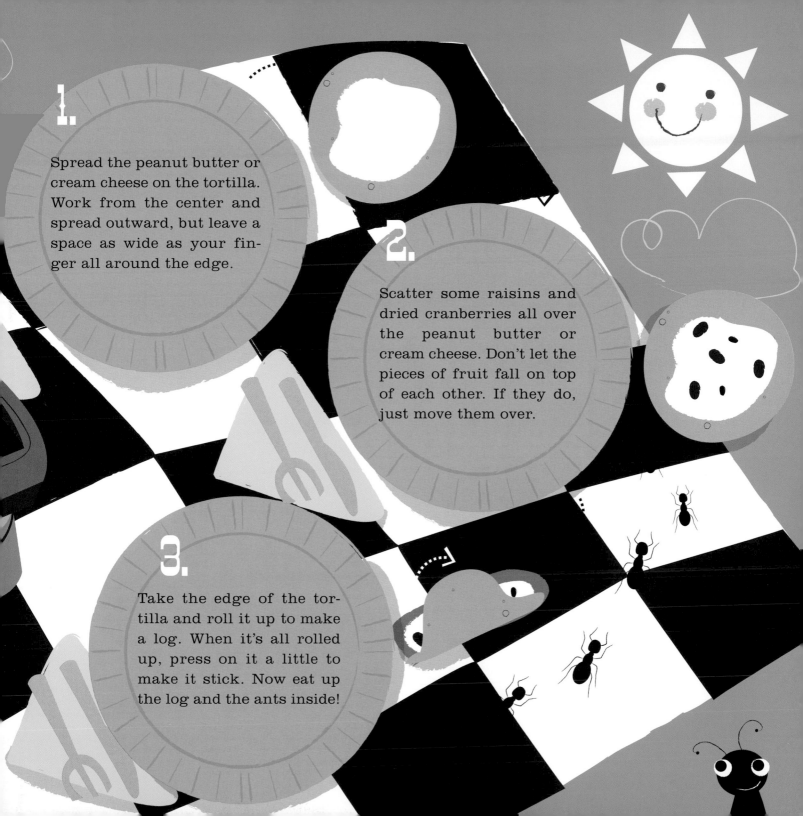

1.

Spread the peanut butter or cream cheese on the tortilla. Work from the center and spread outward, but leave a space as wide as your finger all around the edge.

2.

Scatter some raisins and dried cranberries all over the peanut butter or cream cheese. Don't let the pieces of fruit fall on top of each other. If they do, just move them over.

3.

Take the edge of the tortilla and roll it up to make a log. When it's all rolled up, press on it a little to make it stick. Now eat up the log and the ants inside!

SCREAM FOR ICE CREAM

We all scream for ice cream now and then, but have you ever had ice cream that looked like it might scream back at you?

Ingredients

5 strawberries

2 blueberries

Softened vanilla, chocolate, or strawberry ice cream or frozen yogurt

1 raspberry

Makes 1 screaming dessert treat

Special Tools You Will Need

 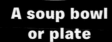 

| An ice-cream scoop | A plastic knife | A soup bowl or plate |

28

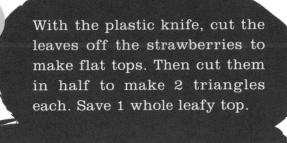

1. With the plastic knife, cut the leaves off the strawberries to make flat tops. Then cut them in half to make 2 triangles each. Save 1 whole leafy top.

weee!

2. Scoop a nice round scoop of ice cream onto a soup bowl or plate. This is the head. Place the strawberries around the ice cream, with the points facing outward. This is a fancy collar. Put the leafy strawberry top on the top of the ice cream. This is the hair.

3. Put the blueberries on the ice cream where the eyes should go. Put the raspberry where the mouth should go. Make sure the little hole in the raspberry faces outward. That's what makes the scream!

Do It Another Way

You can choose any ice-cream flavor that you like. Use other fruits for the face. Use a piece of O-shaped dry cereal for the mouth. Or ask a grown-up to peel and cut a slice of kiwi for you to use as a giant mouth. Then you can use a piece of peel for hair. Just don't eat it!

29

STARRY NIGHT SANDWICHES

Makes 1 open-faced masterpiece

Make a masterpiece on a slice of bread! Some apple butters are spicy, so if you don't care for spice, ask your parents to buy a jar that is just flavored with apples.

Special Tools You Will Need

Hi!

A star-shaped cookie cutter

Measuring spoons

Ingredients

1 slice of your favorite cheese

Super Bread!

1 slice pumpernickel or whole wheat bread

Butter

½ teaspoon of apple butter

1 slice turkey breast

1.

With the cookie cutter, cut out a star from the cheese. (If your cookie cutter is very small, make 2 or 3 stars.)

2.

With the cookie cutter, cut out a star from the turkey breast. (If you've made 2 or 3 cheese stars, do the same with the turkey.)

3.

If you've made large stars, measure ½ teaspoon of apple butter and spoon it onto the center of the bread. Place the turkey star and then the cheese on top of the apple butter.

4.

If you've made small stars, spoon a little apple butter onto 2 or 3 small spots on the bread. Place 1 turkey star on each. Top each with a cheese star. It's edible art!

Do It Another Way

You can use whatever bread you like (call it a Sunshine Sandwich). Use mayonnaise or mustard, or even a spoon of fruit preserves. And if you don't care for turkey, use another lunch meat or just use cheese.

PB 'n' B 'n' H

Makes 4 yummy snacks (or a nice breakfast or lunch)

You've probably had PB 'n' J— peanut butter 'n' jelly. But have you tried PB 'n' B 'n' H? Peanut butter 'n' bananas 'n' honey. Yum!

Special Tools You Will Need

Measuring cup

A shallow soup bowl

A plastic knife

Ingredients

¼ cup of orange juice or apple juice

Honey in a squeeze bottle

4 plain rice cakes (or more if you break any)

Peanut butter, at room temperature (not cold)

1 banana

1.

Measure ¼ cup of juice into the bowl. Peel the banana. Cut it into thin round circles. Put them into the juice. Turn them so the juice coats all sides. Take them out of the juice and set aside.

2.

Carefully spread some peanut butter on the rice cakes. Don't press too hard because they break easily. (If you break one, use another. You can eat up the mistake!)

3.

Drizzle some honey over the peanut butter.

wee!

4.

Put 4 or 5 banana slices on top of each rice cake. Open wide and take a bite!

Do It Another Way

You can use sunflower butter or cottage cheese. Or just use honey and bananas.

Very Veggie Dip

This dip is full of very good things from the vegetable garden.

Makes about 1½ cups of dip

1 cup of regular or low-fat sour cream

½ teaspoon of dried, minced onion (from the spice aisle in the supermarket)

¼ teaspoon of garlic powder

½ medium cucumber, peeled

1 pinch of salt

2 or 3 sprigs of fresh dill or ¼ teaspoon of dried dill

Pita chips

¼ cup of shredded carrot

Ingredients

Special Tools You Will Need

Safety scissors, washed and dried

A plastic knife

Measuring cup and spoons

A dinner plate or tray

A spoon

A small bowl for serving

Do It Another Way

You can make this dip with plain yogurt instead of sour cream. Add 4 or 5 cut-up grape tomatoes if you like.

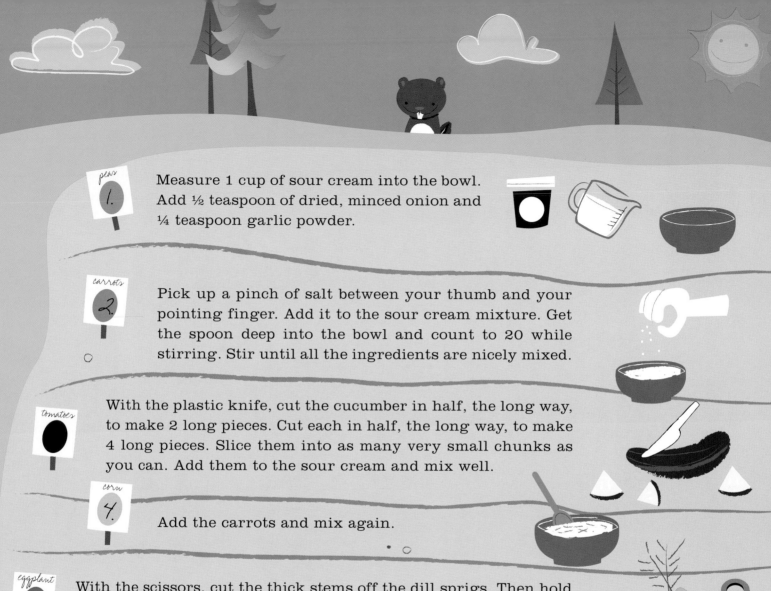

1. Measure 1 cup of sour cream into the bowl. Add ½ teaspoon of dried, minced onion and ¼ teaspoon garlic powder.

2. Pick up a pinch of salt between your thumb and your pointing finger. Add it to the sour cream mixture. Get the spoon deep into the bowl and count to 20 while stirring. Stir until all the ingredients are nicely mixed.

3. With the plastic knife, cut the cucumber in half, the long way, to make 2 long pieces. Cut each in half, the long way, to make 4 long pieces. Slice them into as many very small chunks as you can. Add them to the sour cream and mix well.

4. Add the carrots and mix again.

5. With the scissors, cut the thick stems off the dill sprigs. Then hold the dill leaves over the bowl of dip and cut them into more tiny pieces. They will fall right in. Mix well.

6. Put the bowl onto the dinner plate or tray. Put the pita chips around the bowl. Eat right away!

THE BREAKFAST TRAIN

All aboard the breakfast train! For each car in the train, use 4 mini-muffins. You can make as many cars as you like.
Makes a breakfast buffet for 3 to 4 people

A shallow soup bowl

Measuring cup

3 dinner plates

A plastic knife

Special Tools You Will Need

TICKETS

Ingredients

cheep!

12 mini blueberry or corn muffins

3 or 4 straw-berries

¼ cup of orange juice or apple juice

1 piece of O-shaped dry cereal

6 or 8 frozen melon balls, thawed

3 large bananas

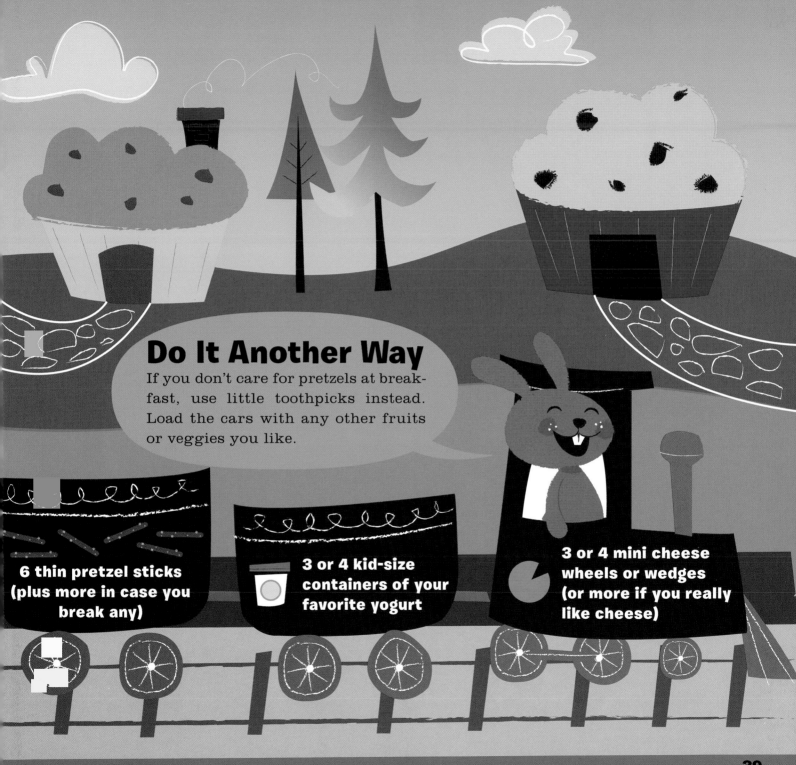

Do It Another Way

If you don't care for pretzels at breakfast, use little toothpicks instead. Load the cars with any other fruits or veggies you like.

6 thin pretzel sticks (plus more in case you break any)

3 or 4 kid-size containers of your favorite yogurt

3 or 4 mini cheese wheels or wedges (or more if you really like cheese)

Train Schedule

1:00

Take the paper wrappers off the muffins. Turn 1 muffin on its side. Find the flat bottom and stick a pretzel into the center. Don't go all the way through. Take another muffin and attach its flat side to the other end of the pretzel stick. Do the same for the rest of the muffins. Now you have the wheels of your train. Carefully put 2 sets of wheels on each plate.

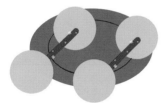

2:00

With the plastic knife, cut the leaves off the strawberries to make flat tops. Then take 1 strawberry and cut off the pointy bottom so it is flat, too. This will be your steam engine strawberry. Set it aside.

3:00

Measure ¼ cup of juice into the bowl. Peel the bananas and cut the curved tips off with the plastic knife to make 3 tube-shaped bananas. Put the tubes and tips into the juice. Turn them so the juice coats all sides. Take them out of the juice and set aside.

4:00

Make sure that each plate has 2 sets of wheels, one behind the other, close enough so that the banana can sit on them. Gently put a banana tube on each set of wheels.

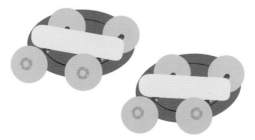

5:00

Line up the plates in the center of the table. The plate at the front of the line will be the steam engine. Place the steam engine strawberry on the side of the banana that is closest to the other plates. Then put the piece of O-shaped cereal on the other end. This is your steam spout.

6:00

Load the other 2 cars of your train by piling 1 melon ball, 1 strawberry half, 1 banana tip, and 1 wheel of cheese on top of each banana tube (or use whatever combination of fruits you like).

7:00

Place any leftover fruit and the yogurt containers on the plates on either side of the train or on small dishes set around it, to make scenery. Next stop, breakfast!